no such thing as thing as over the hill

MAKING THE MOST OF LIFE AFTER 60

JAMES R. KOK

CRC Publications
Grand Rapids, Michigan

Unless otherwise indicated, the Scripture quotations in this publication are from the HOLY BIBLE, NEW INTERNATIONAL VERSION, © 1973, 1978, 1984, International Bible Society. Used by permission of Zondervan Bible Publishers.

No Such Thing as Over the Hill: Making the Most of Life After 60, © 2000 by CRC Publications, 2850 Kalamazoo Ave. SE, Grand Rapids, MI 49560. All rights reserved. With the exception of brief excerpts for review purposes, no part of this book may be reproduced in any manner whatsoever without written permission from the publisher. Printed in the United States of America on recycled paper. ♻

We welcome your comments. Call us at 1-800-333-8300 or e-mail editors@crcpublications.org.

Cover photo: © INDEX STOCK

Library of Congress Cataloging-in-Publication Data
Kok, James R., 1935-
    No such thing as over the hill: making the most of life after 60 / James R. Kok.
      p.   cm.
    ISBN 1-56212-545-1
    1. Aging—United States—Psychological aspects.
    2. Aging—Religious aspects—Christianity. I. Title.
HQ1064.U5 K 65 2000
646.7'0084'6—dc21

00-036090

10 9 8 7 6 5 4 3 2 1

This book is dedicated to
<u>Dr. Barney Steen</u>

Barney Steen entered my life in 1953 when I was starting
my sophomore year at Calvin College. He was the brand-
new varsity basketball coach and Calvin's first director of
physical education. I, an aspiring basketball player, stood
in quiet awe of this important person. Barney led his first
team of young zealots to three league championships.
There were many more to follow. This is not to say I
admired his coaching style personally. He had a bizarre
way of benching me for a while right after I scored a
couple of awesome baskets—maybe he was on to my
tendency to play better when furious. But cannier folk
than I dubbed him a great coach.

Barney and Eleanor have modeled life in the senior years
exceptionally well. They left Calvin, too soon in my
opinion, and started over in Benona County on the shore
of Lake Michigan. In an unknown community they
invested themselves energetically and caringly. There
they earned friendship, respect, and appreciation by
working, playing, and sharing ownership in a growing
rural neighborhood. A new church became their spiritual
home as they discovered Christian kinship with Lutheran
brothers and sisters.

The last time I saw Barney, a year or two ago, we golfed
together near Stony Lake, where the Steens reside now.
Barney's sore hip, since replaced, was aching badly but
he had a unique device to tee up the ball without having to

bend all the way down to the ground. That's Barney. Persisting in spite of pain. Barney always looks for novel ways and fresh slants. He was an accomplished coach and athletic director, but wisdom, insightfulness, and spirit describe him better.

Barney models living in general and senior years in particular like one of God's allstars. I dedicate this book to Barney, my friend, with gratitude and admiration.

CONTENTS

"In your old age I shall still be the same,
when your hair is grey I shall still support you.
I have already done so, I have carried you,
I shall still support and deliver you."

Isaiah 46:4, Jerusalem Bible

INTRODUCTION

*Teach us to number our days aright,
that we may gain a heart of wisdom.*

Psalm 90:12

I jumped at the chance to write about seniors. The audience is huge and the need is clear. After all, being older now means something far different from what it meant in our grandparents' day. Grandmothers these days look as young as their daughters. Grandfathers compete effectively on the golf courses with their grandchildren. Octogenarians are numerous, and many of them are robust. Seniors live in a world with brand-new opportunities and expectations but few up-to-date models to guide them. I thought I could offer a little help.

Then my excitement subsided. I stalled. I thought, What do I know about the issues of elderhood? I lost my confidence. But reality crept in as I realized that for the past fifteen years the bulk of my ministry has been with older folks. Not only that but my parents—ages ninety-one and ninety-six—live nearby and play a prominent role in my daily life. For the last decade and a half we have walked together closely. The final piece countering my qualms about being qualified to write was right under my nose: I am a bona fide oldster! I'm sixty-four. That settled it.

Two separate events stand out in my adult years as eye-openers about the aging process. The first was a family reunion in the Colorado mountains years ago. I was young, in my thirties. We came together from points west, east, and north; singles, families, children, grandparents. All of us enjoyed campfires, marshmallow roasts, hikes, and great food. What I remember most, though, is the moment when my father, about sixty-five, picked up an ax to chop some firewood. It struck fear into our hearts, and several of us moved to stop him. We thought he was too old, too fragile for such strenuous work. We expected a stroke or heart attack to take him down any minute if he lifted the ax.

The second event took place about six months later. I was accepted into a training course in Indianapolis on aging. There I was confronted with the truth about what they called the "Third Age" (meaning the last one-third of our lives). My mind was blown open. Until then, I held every known prejudice, bias, and mistaken idea about seniors. At age thirty-five my understanding of aging received a badly overdue overhaul.

I learned a lot in Indianapolis. The biggest discovery, and most important, was that older people are a contented lot. I learned that, contrary to my youthful stereotype of seniors being defined by sickness, disability, poverty, and depression, the retired describe themselves as being at least as happy as they ever were. And that was thirty years ago. My observation confirms that this is even truer today.

The second major lesson, which I now confirm from my personal experience, was that seniors are physically robust, resilient, and active. Our panic over Dad chopping wood at age sixty-five is embarrassing in its naiveté.

An additional phenomenon popped to the surface. The years we call "senior" can easily equal one-third of our life span. Even for those retiring at a conventional sixty-five, thirty more years of life is not an unrealistic expectation. And for the average fifty-year-old A.A.R.P. enlistee, living to eighty is highly likely.

We live as much of our time in senior years as from birth to age twenty-five or thirty. That is shocking and exciting. A whole new "career" is possible in this Third Age. Opportunities abound. Possibilities await. We Christians must absolutely resist all attitudes that consider the milestone of retirement as the beginning of the end. Such thinking yields a self-fulfilling prophecy. For those who act like retirement is the final curtain, the show is over. Instead, think of retirement as a new birth for a fresh thirty years of life. Even physical death is a birth, a graduation to still another age of growth and satisfying living. Who we are, and what we learn here, I believe, will continue on in some wonderful, mysterious way in the next life.

For most of us the years until retirement can be called the time of productivity. Daily clock punching, child rearing, wage earning, and resource building mark these decades. We are busy supporting our families and other worthwhile institutions like schools, churches, and our communities. Then a new age dawns. When we reach a financial plateau, retirement becomes possible. The less ready can continue, if they choose, with their well-established routines until more comfortably prepared for a different way of life. Those who wish can enter the Third Age.

11

Like finishing high school or college, retirement properly viewed is a commencement, not an ending. As people with a calling from God our pilgrimage changes but does not end. "Rocking chair time" is not an appropriate goal for anybody who is still alive and well. The best prescription for a vital retirement is retiring to new opportunities rather than retiring from the wearisome. Those eager for the freedom to get at projects, start programs, and deepen relationships enter the Third Age healthiest.

Just wanting to quit the tiring routines and take it easy is a prescription for a short retirement. We all know too many whose longed-for years were abbreviated by death. Zestful investment of time and energy in interesting, satisfying activities stretches the mind and regenerates the spirit. Such challenges increase the probability of enjoying a long, satisfying senior era. Retirement must be a looking forward that includes growing and giving.

When he was nearly ninety, Jester Hairston, the well-known gospel musician, actor, and composer, said, "If I knew how young I was when I thought I was old, I would have accomplished a lot more." In his late seventies, Hairston explained, he phased out of some of his interests, thinking his life was nearly over. Fortunately he caught on that he was still abounding in energy, and he resumed a dynamic and productive life. This year he is ninety-nine. Like many of us, Jester Hairston was thrown off track by noticing the number of his years rather than simply continuing to invest in the things he loved.

I recall similar faulty, age-based decision-making in my own life. At age thirty, while serving as the pastor of a church, I mothballed my tennis racquet. It's time, I reasoned, to get serious, to put away childish things and go to work. About ten years later I awakened to the folly of my logic. Still youthful, but emotionally stale and in horrible physical condition, I endeavored to instill balance in my life.

What throws us off is that arbitrary number sixty-five. Ordained by Franklin Delano Roosevelt, not God, the sixty-fifth year has evolved as a watershed that affects us long before we approach it. Ideally there should be no such number posted, just open-ended possibilities as long as we live. Tasks, purpose, participation, relationships, and service must drive us, not preoccupation with how old we are. The Lord honors those with values worth living for.

Personally my aim is determined by my father's long life. Ninety-six and counting. In truth I want to reach at least 100, and expect to. It helps to have a hero's track record to follow, a high goal to reach toward.

The Bible advises us to "number our days" (Ps. 90:12). Total denial of the passing of time is surely inappropriate. We must balance an awareness of life's passing with needed attentiveness to what's really important. A dogged determination to fill every day with worthwhile living plays best.

"Numbering our days" is a call to realize our mortality. When we fail to accurately assess life's limits, we pay a cost. The price we pay is usually a failure to ratchet our friendships up to a meaningful level, neglecting to care for the people we love, to listen to them, to walk alongside them. Knowing there is a terminal point offers a strong incentive to use the gift of time wisely instead of crashing blindly forward. Life is a delicate balance of living fully right to the finish line with a keen awareness of our mortality.

We cannot coast, idle, or drift into healthy senior living. Thoughtful choices must characterize our entry into these senior years, because ours is in many ways a new age. Appropriate living today requires making choices our own parents may not have lived long enough to make. We must chart our courses with little precedent other than a vibrant faith to draw upon.

This book intends to stimulate reflection and intentional behavior for senior living. God-honoring seniors model fresh new ways of living for the younger generation. That takes thought and some risk, as we slip out of our comfort zones and try new things. Because if there is any key to long life, or at least good living, it is continued growth. When mental and physical stimulation stops, life begins to wind down.

The Christian adventure includes a never-ending calling both to enjoy life and to serve others. This prescription for making the world a better place—Kingdom building—will also lead us on a gratifying walk to the beginning of the next age—everlasting life with Jesus.

Seniors
See Better

When I was a child
I talked like a child,
I thought like a child,
I reasoned like a child.

1 Corinthians 13:11

Stereotypes about age are changing rapidly. Old men and women run marathons. The senior golf circuit opens lucrative opportunities for maturing professionals. Even weight-lifting classes for octogenarians fill up.

The point is this: you don't have to stop biking, bowling, or running just because you achieved the status of grandparent or turned sixty-five or seventy-five. You can even, without totally grossing out your neighbors, take up in-line skating after retirement. No one will shame you—that is, unless you crack a wrist.

For most of us, though, aging means phasing out of strenuous exercise and competitive, body-endangering sports. Instead we take up walking, gardening, or swimming laps. These fit well with the changes our bodies signal. Rather than a process of weakening, of losses culminating in death, aging is moving into something new.

The new into which we are moving is, in part, a better and more complete view of life. Vision loss, deafness, illness, and muscular weakness cannot block this opportunity for inner growth. In fact, our losses help us focus on what life is about. Those who see best are not necessarily those who are still skateboarding at seventy-five.

A gift of growing older is the capacity to hold an overview, a broad perspective. The older see the true value of living in this world. Age, seasoned by heartache, clarifies the truly important versus the trivial, the deeply vital over against the superficial. Those whose pilgrimage has been bombed, strafed, and sabotaged are often better able to sort out such truth. The smooth path coveted by all short-circuits a lot of growth into wisdom.

A friend of mine is the mother of two boys, both of whom have tragically died. She has fought on through these circumstances, in the process gaining depth, wisdom, and spiritual brilliance. Clearly her growth has been spurred on by disaster. But "I would give up all gains in a second to have my sons back," she says—a futile hope of one who shines because of the ugliness life has poured over her. To me my friend represents the richness and the ripeness that aging, enhanced by heartbreak, can create.

A pastor I know got off to a fast and successful start after seminary. His churches thrived, and his preaching was acclaimed. He loved to point people faced with tragedy toward the Lord. "Just give it to the Lord," he cried. Then he suffered a stroke. When finally he recovered, he confessed to a friend, "Until I had my stroke, I didn't know what I was talking about."

Older people are a treasure too much disregarded in a productivity-oriented society. We ourselves too easily discount what time has produced in us. Wistful longing for clear vision, for sensitive hearing, and for bounce in our gait can overshadow the spiritual wealth we hold in our own hearts.

A few days ago a handful of my colleagues and I sat with a revered elder statesman, Dr. Harold England, and his wife, Enid. Hungrily we peppered them with questions, enticing them to share stories from their rich, long ministry. We treasured every crumb they dropped. But another thing happened too. It always does. When seniors talk of their pilgrimage, they sparkle. Remembering is life-giving to those who listen and to those who tell.

It is easy for our youth-oriented society to miss the treasures that abound in the form of older citizens. And it's easy for seniors to discount themselves when the quick and sleek seem to handle a complex world with apparent ease.

The best perspective sees the gifts of all ages. Discount nobody. Shelve no one. Because each person in his or her own way sheds light on something. Each is a beloved child of God to be treasured.

Questions for Reflection

1. "Rather than a process of weakening, of losses culminating in death, aging is moving into something new." What "new" things have you moved into during your senior years?

2. What are some ways our society could benefit from valuing the perspective attained by its older citizens?

3. "Our losses help us focus on what life is about." Do you agree or disagree? What spiritual gains have you have achieved through the losses you've experienced?

Seniors Should Major in Love

And now I will show you the most excellent way.

1 Corinthians 12:31

I am anticipating attending a two-day event in Albuquerque for clinically trained pastors. The American Red Cross is preparing a team to coordinate spiritual care in response to airline disasters. When I first received the invitation, my prompt inner voice said no. I did not relish spending the time away from home. A couple of eight-hour classes for something I probably would never use sounded wearisome. Fortunately I recovered from my rush of inertia and applied for admittance.

The Albuquerque event, I realized, is a metaphor for senior years. Two opposing forces are vying with each other. On the one hand the attraction and delight of new growth and experiences entice me. Countering this attraction is the strong pull of the comfortable and familiar. Staying where I am is itself delightful. (*Warning:* When the pleasures of remaining in the comfort zone always outweigh the joys of growth, life starts ending.) In the end, good sense convinced me I should join the airline disaster training. Reason overruled my body's cries for comfort and ease.

As my years add up, the fight between these forces grows more intense. The delights and joys of comfort and security clamor louder, win more easily. Sound thinking must continue to win a share of these battles. Otherwise the delights of stretching and growing will fade away with inevitable negative consequences—spiritual shrinkage.

Trying the fresh and unknown is not merely delightful; it is life-enhancing. The human brain continues to regenerate itself as long as it receives lively stimulation. The work of solving and discovering is life giving. The more actively engaged the brain stays, the greater will be the overall well-being of the whole person.

Retirement years open the doors to realizing some unfulfilled ambitions and desires. Only rarely should they be just "more of the same."

As I think ahead, I intend to continue in a lot of the same grooves as elderhood ripens. For instance, take my work as a pastor. Advancing years qualify me more for pastoral work. Dropping out now feels wrong, even wasteful. So I plan to continue indefinitely while trimming off some of the excesses, eliminating the things that block fresh challenges. Three or four opportunities beckon:

- I would like to golf a little more than I do now. Maybe eighteen holes a week instead of nine. Nine holes a week has felt like staying just barely semi-competent, a step away from consistency, a dozen steps from excellence.

- Another goal hanging in the closet of my fantasies is to fish in the lakes and streams of the Eastern Sierra Mountains. The pleasant drive to those gorgeous locations, combined with the satisfaction of getting good at enticing trout to my hook, lures me strongly.

- A third task for the decades ahead is writing. Now I squeeze it in. I anticipate ample space for daily creativity. There is much I still ache to share.

As I concluded spelling out these objectives for my future, a surprising Bible verse literally popped into my mind. At first it seemed irrelevant. Then it emerged as powerfully appropriate. The verse is the last sentence of 1 Corinthians, chapter 12: "And now I will show you the most excellent way." The fantastic teaching on love in chapter 13 follows.

Wham! It hit me dead center. My goals, modest and possible as they are, include nothing about relationships. In typical male fashion, measurable accomplishments mark my goals. Not only that, but I can carry out each of these goals by myself. They will gratify me, just me.

"The most excellent way" to retire is to give love. All kinds of helpful, valuable, profitable services surround us all the time, says Paul. Although golfing, fishing, and writing are fine, I need something more. Easily discounted or overlooked, love is supremely valuable. Giving love must top my agenda.

Maybe love-giving should define our senior years more than anything else. Here lies an uncluttered span of years. We have an opportunity to step away from worrying about achievement and maintaining productivity. Instead, we can give ourselves.

When my elderly father lamented his lack of being needed, I thought, but didn't express, my protest: "I need you. I would like you to be interested in me, to express encouragement, to congratulate me for my accomplishments. Show overt appreciation for my involvement in your life." Multiply that need times the other nine children; add a dozen grandchildren and a handful of great-grandchildren. There sits a full-time job for any senior citizen. The need for love is inexhaustible. A long line of hungry souls stands waiting.

Love defines the responsibility of our senior years. Shower gifts of compliments, hugs, kindness, and endorsement on the hungry, unsure, younger folks. This is the better way. Much better. Fishing, golfing, writing, please step aside. Let love lead the way.

Questions for Reflection

1. What are some of the ways we can avoid "spiritual shrinkage"?

2. Take a quick inventory of your lifestyle. Do your activities and goals include affirming others? Think of some specific ways you can show love to those around you.

3. How do retirement years offer a unique opportunity to follow Paul's "most excellent way"?

Self-Centered Behavior Cheats the Young

I will not let you go unless you bless me.

Genesis 32:26

When my book *90% of Helping Is Just Showing Up* lay in my hand for the first time, my excitement soared. Not quite as high as it did for the births of our children, but up there in the same stratosphere. In fact, the satisfaction felt similar to giving birth to a child, as I can only imagine it.

Soon after this peak experience, I had an opportunity to visit with a retired pastor whom I know very well and call on often. With modulated enthusiasm I presented him with my baby. He took it, glanced quickly at the cover, said thank you, and set it aside. "I never published," he said, and went on to speak for a few minutes about ideas he had at one time considered putting together for a book. I listened, politely resigned that the tables had been turned. My good news was like bad news to him. He wanted to talk about his disappointments. To him my accomplishment registered zero.

A few weeks later I stopped in again. As was my habit, in between listening to my friend, I shared pieces of what was going on in my life. This time I added that I had been invited to lead a workshop training volunteers in a nearby church he knew well. His response fit what I had come to anticipate: "Well, they never ask me to do anything."

Over the years I have noticed this sad pattern popping up in visits with others as well. It seems to show up especially in those who have in fact contributed a great deal to society. These folks have given a lot but now seem sadly disheartened about their dwindling influence and the goals they never reached. They give up center stage reluctantly and conjure up little interest or joy in others' accomplishments.

My father, age ninety-six, also a retired pastor, shocked me recently with a lament over being unknown and unneeded in the church. Both are true in a literal sense. He is known by a shrinking handful, and his days of leadership are long over. Aging always takes us out of the mainstream of popularity and usefulness. So why was I shocked? Because I expected that by the age of ninety-six my father would have made peace with the realities and losses of advanced age. I didn't think it would still be bothering him twenty-five years after stepping down.

Maybe pastors inherit a bigger loss than most as they age away from the central roles they long held. But each of us inches into our senior years having to unload many armloads of privilege, power, and popularity.

An inner sense of worth helps counteract the losses inevitable with the passing of the years. A realization of our high value based on God's positive regard and the love of our family serves as a strong antidote to the empty feelings that may accompany our decreased productivity.

We have to know our worth in our souls and experience it through the conspicuous ongoing love of family or friends. We thrive best with God's "You are my beloved" carved into our hearts and the active support of kinfolk.

A sure prescription for sadness is pinning our value on tangible accomplishments and possessions. They fade. They dissipate. The only lasting investments that satisfy the soul indefinitely are good relationships—with the Lord and with people. When such sustenance nourishes our soul we are better equipped to handle our own losses. Satisfying relationships enable us to congratulate and celebrate with the younger generation as they achieve new heights.

But regardless of the heartiness of our relationships, we need to do more. What's called for is an eyes-open determination to fight preoccupation with self. Self-centeredness may be a natural pitfall for seniors; if so, it calls for thoughtful opposition every day. How? By intentionally taking joy in another's victory. By deliberately quieting personal fear of shrinkage. And by celebrating the milestones reached by others.

Achieving senior citizen status does not revoke our spiritual obligation to encourage others. In fact, just the opposite is true. I sought a paternal pat on the head from the man to whom I gave my book. Instead I received a lament over his own disappointments. As older folks, we're revered far more than we realize. Our new role includes blessing the coming generations while playing down our own receding importance. A hearty "Well done" from a revered elder is like vitamins for a younger soul. Senior citizens must engrave on their minds the fact that younger folks hunger for a blessing. That's one gift a shaky hand, a tired body, a forgetful mind can always offer. Encouraging another is a lifelong opportunity for doing good.

Questions for Reflection

1. The author states that those who have contributed a great deal to society sometimes have the hardest time "giving up center stage." Has this been true in your experience?

2. Do you agree that self-centeredness may be a natural pitfall for seniors? Why is it so easy to slip into as we grow older?

3. Recall gifts of compliments or other affirmation you have received from significant people in your life. What difference did it make to you?

4. "We thrive best with God's 'You are my beloved' carved on our hearts." How does knowing our value lies in our relationship to God free us to bless others?

Somebody's Watching You

Set an example . . . in speech, in life,
in love, in faith and in purity.

1 Timothy 4:12

When Marilyn was in her teens, her young brother and sister died tragically. The devastation deeply affected Marilyn's whole family. It changed them permanently.

Decades later, her own parental years past, Marilyn speaks of how she watched her mother. "I intentionally observed how she carried on in the aftermath of losing two children. I wanted to know how survival looks, how it is done."

Marilyn adds one amazing memory. She recalls her mother habitually waking her up in the morning with a cheery "Get up, dear, it's another beautiful day." A surprising lesson for Marilyn's study of her mother's grief.

What Marilyn did consciously is happening all the time. Presently our own family is observing our parents as they inch along at ninety-six and ninety-one, continuing to participate in life's opportunities. We are learning how it can be done. Dad takes a daily one-mile walk. Mother watches *Jeopardy* religiously. Together they start the day with a video of favorite hymns. Devotions accent every meal. They dress attractively and attend church services faithfully. And so they continue—blowing our minds with new awareness of the possibilities of extreme old age.

We have also become aware that we are being watched. Especially my wife, Linda, now nearly three years post-mastectomy. Comments still trickle in about how smoothly she managed that major challenge—chemotherapy, reconstruction, and all. Her practical, matter-of-fact approach, whimper-free, set a healthy standard that was noticed by colleagues and friends who may travel that road themselves someday.

The biblical admonition to "set a good example" never becomes outdated. We are always watching and being watched until and including our dying day.

I have noticed that my parents' activities opened ideas for me. Some of what they did gave me a kind of permission or a nudge in a new direction. Their venturesome tourism, while modest, sparked that possibility for me. Had they never embarked for distant places I may never have considered such adventures for myself. I might have figured that travel is for other people.

My father loved mountain climbing and camping. Most of the family gravitated naturally to similar pastimes. Near age sixty I climbed Yosemite's Half Dome because Dad had decades earlier.

Both of my parents had attractive penmanship. I recall aspiring to join their team. Writing with classical beauty still eludes me, but from childhood on the example they unknowingly set has inspired me, even in my handwriting.

At age sixty-four, a third of my life may lie ahead. I view it as an opportunity to enjoy all the benefits senior years offer. But it calls for just a teeny bit of conscious modeling as well, modeling for our children about making these years rich and rewarding. Conventional routines may dominate our scene. But here and there we plot a little coloring outside the lines to sabotage the younger generation's stereotypes about older folks. I have a friend who took up motorcycle riding after he turned sixty-six. Surely that caught his kids' attention and taught them something. Not only is he living out an old ambition, he is pushing aside outdated notions about sixty-plus people and permanently changing his own children's thinking for the better.

Positive modeling makes the world a better place, but even bad examples can be turned to good. Turned-off youth can resolve to do the exact opposite of ill-tempered, overly cautious, or insensitive parents.

I recall a picnic I attended with a friend's family when I was a college student. A storm was bearing down on us with a reservoir of rain about to drop. The wind was howling; the food rapidly chilling. The father insisted that we gather for the prayer of blessing on the food. A lengthy grace followed, and the "Amen" seemed to pull the trigger for the downpour. Better, I thought in my irritation, to call out, "Grab the food and pray as you eat!" The father's modeling sent a strong message of priorities, but overdone piety cools godly ardor.

My wife and I strive mightily to leave happy memories of times together with our three grandchildren. Their parents, our children, received, for a variety of reasons, a neutral response from their grandparents. Following our parents' example would perpetuate a tradition of detachment and indifference. We are clearly reacting against passive modeling by leaning hard in the opposite direction.

One of my favorite pastimes today is writing. Until I was forty years old, I had not met and known an author. Then I became a colleague of Rev. Ralph Heynen at Pine Rest Christian Hospital. Ralph wrote books. Without a doubt his modeling opened the possibility in my mind. Maybe I can do that, I thought.

Someone is watching. God watches us and sustains us in adversity. Children, grandchildren, and others watch us to see how to live. This living to show the way is an awesome challenge, one that's never finished. But by modeling a realistic and credible life—in matters of body, mind, and spirit—throughout our time on this earth, we can empower the next generation.

Questions for Reflection

1. Think about your own interests and attitudes. How were they affected by your parents?

2. Name others who have inspired you by their example—either positive or negative—to venture beyond your natural comfort zone.

3. What do you think about the author's suggestion that seniors sabotage their families' stereotypes about old age by "coloring outside the lines"? What kind of activities would you consider doing that would fall under this category?

4. How can seniors model "a credible and realistic life—in matters of body, mind, and spirit" for their children? Give some examples.

A Harsh Blow
May Cripple
Your Spirit

*We do not lose heart. Though outwardly
we are wasting away, yet inwardly
we are being renewed day by day.*

2 Corinthians 4:16

The body ages. My spirit stays young," claims a friend of mine. His conclusion feels accurate to me. But further pondering finds me wondering if my friend is really right.

This much I do know: My body is not the same as when I was twenty-two. Limitations and weaknesses, then unknown, now call attention to themselves daily. I walk well, but running is a joke. Even throwing a stone over-handed feels silly. Back then my blood pressure was a classic 120/80. Now, with medication, it averages 145/86.

My spirit, however, feels better than ever. Forty years ago, during my twenties, little more played on the screen of my mind than physical activities and wants. I felt hungry. Today I am filled with the treasures of love and friendship. The delights of nature, music, the garden, and grand-children nourish my soul. Sorrows, reminiscence, and nostalgia richly season my previously insensitive spirit. I feel spiritually wealthy.

Right now I can say yes to my friend's assertion. My spirit thrives as my body weakens. In fact, they appear to be heading in opposite directions. Spirit up. Body down. I resonate with Paul's diagnosis: "Inwardly we are being renewed day by day."

My suspicion that the spirit may, in fact, sometimes weaken springs from too many encounters with unhappy seniors. Their spirit does not seem to be renewed. These folks sing a song of discouragement, cheerlessness, even impatience with life. They advertise old age as a steady downward slide in all respects. Listening to these people, the hope of "daily renewal" seems not to be all-inclusive.

Before he died, Grant, a candidate for "sainthood," suffered physical pain that was made sharply worse by pangs of doubt. During his life, Grant maximized the goodness of God and celebrated God's gracious gift of salvation through Jesus Christ. He taught it, preached it, exuded it. But as Grant's body weakened, his spirit lost confidence. From the radiant proclamation of amazing grace, Grant slipped down to a state of trembling uncertainty.

This too-common loss of spiritual confidence seems to contradict my friend's claim that bodies weaken but spirits do not. Obviously discouragement does settle on some of God's children.

Just think of Job. Man of God that he was, Job struggled desperately with God when the family he loved and his possessions were taken away. Battered by unimaginable heartbreak, Job cried, "My spirit is broken; my days are extinct; the grave is ready for me." Job's grief was pulling him toward death. A broken spirit does not necessarily go hand in hand with renewal.

Grant and Job sank when their health was taken away. That's reality—spirit and body are tightly woven together. Crushing blows to the one can drag down the other.

But the gradual weakening of the body we all experience can be accommodated without spiritual depression. Runners can learn to walk. Those who are vigorous can learn to enjoy more sedentary pastimes. And most often, those who ease into these changes have a positive attitude. More than 80 percent of folks over sixty-five name these as the best years of their lives, in spite of physical weakening.

Even though our spirit may not age, we continue to be vulnerable to the dispiriting blasts of grief and loss as long as we live. And sharp blasts can knock joy and satisfaction for a major loss.

When their brilliant, effervescent, sixty-year-old son died unexpectedly from an aneurysm, Fred and Betty slid into a deep hole. Little mattered. Their light had gone out. Lively no longer, their faces and bodies sagged. Their good health eroded. Like Job, they were heartbroken; they seemed to be on a path to the grave. Their clouded vision now saw a loving God only dimly, through a heavy fog. For Fred and Betty, the inward renewal described by Paul in 2 Corinthians seemed to be sidelined.

Is it possible to build spiritual muscles that stay strong while illness wracks our body and drains our life? Can we acquire a kind of spiritual insurance to block depression after tornadoes sweep our dearest loves away? Such insurance, if available, would exact too high a price from us; a system that would keep our spirits consistently high in the face of serious loss would require us to give up our humanity.

I once asked a group of recently bereaved adults, "If I could supply you with a pill that would remove your sorrow, would you take it?" Their answer was no. They realized that their pain was inextricably wound up with their lost loved one. Eradicating their heartache would mean taking away their memories and further removing their dear one. They had discovered that pain and joy belong together; love and grief are a package. Spiritual depression temporarily fit their situation.

For the most part, then, my friend was right. Our spirit stays young even as our body grows old. When we live a balanced life, when our setbacks are moderate, we may experience spiritual vitality. But if we get hit by a freight train, our sense of spiritual well-being will slide downhill fast. The good news: God holds us even when we can't feel his embrace.

So when extreme weakness and trembling debility overtake my body, I pray for a seed of awareness to persist that I am safe in the arms of Jesus.

Questions for Reflection

1. Looking back, is your outlook on life improving with the passing of time? Deteriorating? About the same?

2. How would you answer the question "If I could supply you with a pill that would remove your sorrow, would you take it?" Why or why not?

3. What circumstances, opportunities, and people contribute most to the renewal of your spirit day by day?

A Plain Wrapper Chapter for Married Couples

There is a time for everything,
and a season for every activity
under heaven: . . . a time to embrace. . . .

Ecclesiastes 3:1, 5

Sex is important. But it is not as important as some think. Living well without sexual activity has been demonstrated by countless exemplary human beings. Unlike food and water, sex is not essential to our physical survival. Multitudes live apart from sexual intimacy—some by choice, others by circumstance. They live well anyway.

But sex is important to a relationship. Important, not essential. Sex offers to a marriage a sweet seasoning not easily acquired in another way.

Older folks, lower on testosterone and estrogen, need to work at keeping that seasoning alive in their marriage. Sexual intimacy is a gift of God to be valued, appreciated, and enjoyed by married couples as long as possible. Although we can live without it, sexual pleasure, like music or like beauty in art or in nature, fits into the category of higher gifts that add intangible spiritual qualities to our lives.

For a variety of reasons, sexual activity often drops by the wayside as the years multiply. Explanations range from tiredness to depression, from hormonal changes to diminished desire. Some older folks think of sex as an activity of youth or just feel it is unseemly for senior citizens. Now and then illness or injury interrupts the customary routines. When that happens, inertia may set in and sex may be shelved—sometimes permanently.

Most men and women are shy about sex. Initiating lovemaking is seldom easy. Such intimacy awes men and women even as it beckons strongly. The unique personalness of sex intimidates both spouses sharply. Making an overture to come together constitutes an ego risk not easily taken. Hesitation or coolness, real or imagined, even a perceived weariness, can constitute a confidence-shattering rejection. So it's easy to understand how the delicacy and fragility that permeates the area of intimacy may gradually provoke calling off the dance altogether.

Ralph and Betty's times of sexual togetherness slowly dropped in frequency as they inched toward seniorhood. By ages fifty-five and fifty-three they no longer came together sexually. Both admitted, when they looked back, that they missed this part of their life. And both pinpointed fear of rejection as the reason for the passive negligence that allowed this unhappy cessation.

A Christian speaker at Ralph and Betty's church facilitated the end of their sad stalemate. In a burst of self-revelation, she offered the simple solution that revived intimacy in her own marriage: Schedule sex.

Putting sex on the calendar violates the common notion that sex should emerge as the culmination of a romantic scenario. "Schedule sex!" some will no doubt object. "Schedule sex! That is totally unromantic. Spontaneity makes for intimacy as it is supposed to be."

Maybe so. But even with highly energized younger couples, some degree of scheduling guarantees that even the tired, who easily assent to postponement, will come together regularly.

For the senior set scheduling sex can work wonders, as it did for Ralph and Betty. On the drive home that night, Betty took the initiative. "I think we should try scheduling," she said quietly. "It's OK with me," Ralph responded. "You say when." Presto, their years-long stalemate was broken. They quickly agreed on a weekend evening. Now well into their sixties, the formula holds effectively.

I have shared this story with a couple of dozen marriage partners. Some had been caught by the challenge of timing—when one was ready the other was not. Others let sex slide because of the risk of rejection. A few were actually not getting along well but agreed to schedule intimacy anyway. Overall, the results have been positive. Most of these couples were able to resume their sexual life. Even those who put sex on the calendar in spite of friction between them reported positive results. Physical intimacy broke through some of the hard feelings that talking merely set in stone. Their willingness to schedule intimacy demonstrated the principle "Act loving and you will feel loving." The idea that you have to feel loving before you can act loving too often stymies resolution of conflict or tension and easily prolongs estrangement.

One of the myths of aging holds that sexual activity ceases in the senior years. The truth is, it may fade in direct correlation to other physical weakening. Physical weakening, we now know, can be countered by being active—either continuing an active life or beginning later on in life.

But even more crucial than physical condition is attitude. With an awareness of the goodness of sexual intimacy and the intention of keeping sexual intimacy alive, married partners can enjoy a long, pleasurable life together—until death finally parts them.

Questions for Reflection

1. Why do so many people feel that sex is unseemly for seniors?

2. "Putting sex on the calendar violates the common notion that sex should emerge as the culmination of a romantic scenario. . . . 'Spontaneity makes for intimacy as it is supposed to be.'" Do you agree or disagree? Why?

3. "Even more crucial than physical condition is attitude." What is your attitude toward sexual intimacy in your marriage?

Growth
Requires Effort

Do not conform any longer to the
pattern of this world, but be transformed
by the renewing of your mind.

Romans 12:2

G eorge, eighty, called and asked if I would visit him in his hospital room. He wanted to share an exciting experience. Although his prognosis was poor—he had only weeks, maybe months to live—George decided to take a step he'd never taken. Lying in his hospital bed, George, a lifelong Christian, decided to directly ask Jesus to enter his life. So he closed his eyes and silently spoke these simple words of invitation: "Jesus, please come into my heart."

"I'm changed," George reported happily. "I've always been cranky, crabby, and hot-tempered. All of that is gone now. I do not feel the same. I'm a new man. I'm at peace."

This revolution in George's spirit held even as his weakened body slipped closer and closer to the end forecast by the medical folks. Death came, but George died serenely. In a unique way he had put his house in order. He had sought a fix in his soul rather than additional time. Even as his sick body wasted away, George was well. He achieved dramatically and tardily what all of us covet—the spiritual tranquility that enables us to override the inevitable bumps and storms of life.

George is an exception, though. Most people die the way they live. Seldom do people change much, even as the curtain comes down. Crabby folks stay crabby. The easygoing keep going easy. Loners die alone and relational people exit with their friends close at hand. Contrary to conventional notions, deathbed transformations rarely happen.

If anything, aging produces more of the same in people. Stubbornness hardens. Generosity expands. Devoutness deepens. Competitive people just play different games with new intensity. While aging may mellow some folks a little, that is mostly a myth; certainly it's unusual enough not to depend on. Unless change and growth are intentionally sought and earnestly engineered, they are not apt to occur.

For those who are willing to stretch, though, the rewards are great. Take Bea, for instance. She worked as an established medical professional for many years. Then, at age sixty-one, thirsty for spiritual nutrition, Bea stepped out to find what she was missing. She added theological seminary courses to her load. These days Bea radiates excitement about her discoveries. This adventure has added so much depth to her life that she wishes she'd embarked on it decades earlier. As Bea's eligibility for Social Security approaches, a second career in ministry entices her.

Few of us grab the golden ring of serenity as close to the finish line as George did. Few find a fresh spiritual place, sweet and calm, so near the end of life. Nor can many follow Bea's path, lining up for degrees in theology. But all of us can grow. Our growth depends on our willingness to take moderate risks. Venturesomeness breaks down barriers and opens new doors into the exciting challenges of the unknown. George tiptoed in to where he'd never been before. He moved a long way while hardly flexing a muscle. Bea sneaked apprehensively into a whole new world, paying tuition and writing papers. Her venture required massive exertion.

God urges us toward lifelong renewal and growth—until we take our last breath. "Be transformed by the renewing of your mind," said the apostle Paul. He knew the key to staying truly alive: our understanding, our ideas, our breadth of experience must continue to grow. An active mind sends health to the whole body.

The catchy U.S. Army recruiting slogan "Be all that you can be" is worth applying to all of life. A smorgasbord of opportunities surrounds seniors. Some of these require little effort; others may call for stepping out of well-established routines. For those who are able, travel beckons. And when literal travel is no longer possible, television and videotapes can offer the thrills of travel from the comfort of home. Books, periodicals, and magazines are often reasonably priced or available free at the local library. Stimulating concerts, lectures, fairs, conferences, and Bible studies surround us. The challenges of hobbies excite some seniors; volunteering in familiar or unfamiliar places stretches others. Still others consciously expand their friendship circles, welcoming the unexpected treasures offered by people of different outlooks and heritage.

After forty years of employment and homemaking, Ben and Sarah speak passionately about their new challenges as docents in an area museum. They personally identify with the museum and display a sense of ownership that heightens their enthusiasm. In retirement, Ben and Sarah are healthier than ever.

It's true that people are not all the same. Contentment seems to come easily to some folks as they move in well-worn grooves. As a rule, though, sameness soon blinds us to our surroundings, no matter how interesting we found them originally.

During my days as a hospital pastor I drove a well-defined, seven-mile route to my office for many years. One day I needed to ride with a colleague. We traveled the exact route I had taken day in and day out. But this time I was sitting in the passenger seat. To my surprise, I saw things I had never noticed. That minor change ushered in previously unseen sights and objects.

Praising the Lord afresh and singing new songs of the wonders of our gracious God flow from taking on new challenges and sailing uncharted waters. Sometimes staying on a familiar path may serve a valuable purpose, but choosing a deliberate detour enables us to discover the surprises along the way. For there we meet God anew.

Questions for Reflection

1. What is it that keeps you from trying new things? How can you break down that barrier (or barriers)?

2. Make a short list of "deliberate detours"— experiences that might pull you out of well-worn grooves into new discoveries. Commit to trying at least one of them in the weeks ahead.

3. "Aging produces more of the same in people. Stubbornness hardens. Generosity expands. Devoutness deepens." Do you agree? Is it possible to change the patterns we establish early on in life?

4. Do you imagine that growth continues in the next life in Christ's presence? In what ways might we continue to grow?

Advantages of Aging

God heard the boy crying. . . .

Genesis 21:17

It may come as a surprise to the young, but I've discovered that aging has significant advantages. One of these is an increasing capacity to see the big picture. Growing older clears away the underbrush and allows us to focus on the essentials.

Here's an example. Today, on the threshold of sixty-five, I can summarize the Bible quite simply: "God created a perfect universe. Human beings messed it up. God heard their cries and saved them."

At age forty-five, my synopsis of the gospel message differed greatly. Back then I wove complex and elaborate details into a long tapestry of explanation. I explored numerous side roads and tangents on the journey toward understanding. Even the most interested parties wearied of listening to me.

Now I see that a small verse from the book of Genesis presents a metaphor for understanding the entire gospel drama. Hagar and her infant son, Ishmael, expelled from Abraham's compound, face death in the desert. The anguished mother lays the wailing child down and goes a distance away to wait for his death. Helplessly she sits and cries. Then, the writer says, "God heard the boy crying." Angelic help soon arrives. He is saved! She is saved! That says it all. Uninvited help is offered to lost humanity. A God touched by personal distress moves to save. The gospel captured in a nutshell!

I relish this powerful, condensed version of a responsive, tenderhearted God who rescues his people. Others may color in supportive details, but this brief, heartwarming good news satisfies me.

Another example. The tragic high school shootings in Littleton, Colorado, triggered a nationwide outpouring of intense reflection. I sat with a group of mostly younger pastors one day, pondering the horror of it all. The majority opinion, expressed by a variety of people, went something like this: "God allows such things to awaken a decaying morality." My minority report trimmed things back to this kernel of truth: "People destroy. Victims cry. God feels our hurts; God lifts and restores."

Along with this ability to see things simply and clearly comes another delicious side effect to growing older: a diminishing dependence on the approval of others. I am still conscious, as I write theological ideas, of all the brilliant minds ready to disassemble my naive sentences. Slight apprehension registers in my solar plexus about their assessment, but not enough to derail me. Fifteen years ago, it would have. Today I believe confidently and passionately the simple truths I hold. Fear of others' disapproval no longer controls my actions. What produced this change? Little else but age.

But I've also observed a downside in this relative indifference to what others think. Several decades ago, while I was serving as an intern pastor at a large university hospital, a retired Episcopal priest volunteered in our pastoral care department. Each day when greeting him I noticed the unshaven hairs under his nose. Back then I thought he was incredibly careless. Today I understand —it really didn't matter to him. A quick shave, and he was on his way. Public opinion no longer pushed him to meticulous grooming. Other things were more important. My youthful judgment, I realize now, too easily discredited the man for his superficial flaws.

Shrinking regard for others' approval elevates confidence. But it can also open the door to slovenly habits. Unpressed pants and coffee-stained sweaters may not concern those who are past the daily commute to work, but others may judge internal wisdom by external appearance. And although it's true that packaging isn't everything, it does make a difference. Fortunately the Lord looks past crumbs and coffee spills.

Two blessings, then, stand out as we age: a capacity to see the big picture and freedom from being controlled by the need for others' approval. While the young frantically plan, produce, and engineer, seniors seasoned by age and experience see more clearly what truly matters—how beloved they are by God.

As the complexities of doctrine and technology multiply during our senior years, our understanding of this simple truth comforts and strengthens us. Such knowledge frees us from our fears, allowing us to rest in God's sweet peace and secure embrace.

Questions for Reflection

1. How does growing older "clear away the underbrush" and enable us to see more clearly "the big picture"?

2. Has your understanding of the gospel changed over the years? In what way?

3. Do you agree with the author's claim that one of the blessings of aging is freedom from being controlled by the need for approval? What are you less self-conscious about now compared to when you were younger?

Know When to Hold 'Em, Know When to Fold 'Em

Abraham fell facedown; he laughed and said to himself, "Will a son be born to a man a hundred years old? Will Sarah bear a child at the age of ninety?"

Genesis 17:17

I was stunned when sixty-five-year-old Herman declined renomination as an elder in his church because he had reached the "official" age of retirement. "I've done my church work," he argued. "It's time now to enjoy life. That's what retirement means— moving on to leisure years." To my way of thinking, sixty-five looks like the time to begin such service in earnest. Not time to quit.

After all, retirement is likely to open Herman's schedule, not restrict it. Besides, for many people, age sixty-five marks the consolidation of such worthy attributes as credibility, perspective, wisdom, depth, understanding, patience, and spiritual maturity. It's the wrong time to move into a life of inactivity.

That reminds me of an anecdote shared by Paul Tournier, M.D. Tournier wrote about a pastor of whom it was said, "He was such a warm and friendly person, until he retired." That man, like our reluctant elder, shows serious gaps in his perspective on what it means to live a Christ-like life. Both acted as though there are term limits on Christian servanthood and kindness.

On the other hand, there's Joe. Joe is a volunteer Bible teacher at his church. His adult class is over thirty members strong. This is Joe's twenty-third year of teaching; he's shooting for twenty-five. But at seventy-seven years old, repetitiveness and lapses of memory are beginning to plague his weekly presentations. Even though his class is beginning to murmur about his failing acuity, they will not ask Joe to resign. In deference to his years of leadership, they continue to attend faithfully. Joe's wife notices his difficulties, and she pushes futilely for his retirement. He's determined to go for twenty-five years, slippage or no slippage.

Kenny Rogers's great country-western song, "You gotta know when to hold 'em, know when to fold 'em; know when to walk away, know when to run," presents a relevant metaphor for the dilemma of senior years. Knowing "when to fold 'em" is something seniors need to discover for themselves. One person should go longer, another not as long. So how do we decide? Rather than base our decisions on our own arbitrary notions or personal whims, we need to ask ourselves, What does God want?

Finding out what God wants isn't always easy. Still, some answers are simple enough. For instance, if Herman had asked himself that question, he might have realized that

God doesn't want us to stop serving in the church simply because we reach some arbitrary age—whether it's sixty-five, seventy, or seventy-five. God wants us to serve as long as we can make a contribution. Most of the time, the believing community can assess this best.

Likewise, it seems clear that God doesn't expect people to keep on serving past the point of effectiveness. Joe's desire to be recognized for twenty-five years of service in the church isn't a good enough reason to continue teaching. Joe would do well to consider his wife's judgment and seek the advice of trusted friends rather than press on with tunnel-vision determination.

Today more than ever, our culture allows and encourages people to develop their gifts. To the extent that men and women can use their gifts on the basis of what they have to offer instead of being limited by age, race, or gender, this freedom seems consistent with the spirit of God. It appropriately opens doors to everybody. It gives us room for spiritual growth.

This freedom for making personal choices also introduces unprecedented challenges. Knowing when to stop, when to step aside, and when to let someone else step front and center requires wisdom and discernment. To increase the odds of getting it right, we need to exercise careful spiritual discretion and seek the wisdom of seasoned colleagues. We need to be prayerfully sensitive to what the situation calls for. And when the time does come to relinquish our role, we need to pray for the courage to step down gracefully.

Seniors hold a reservoir of experience, wisdom, creativity, depth, patience, maturity, and love. For that reason, "rocking chair" thinking is a major waste for the majority of those past sixty. It's better to use the gifts God gave us as long as we can. Then, when the time comes to step aside, we'll be ready.

Questions for Reflection

1. Why do people retire early? What factors influenced (or will influence) your own decision to retire?

2. What are some ways we can discern God's will for our lives?

3. According to the author, "'Rocking chair' thinking is a major waste for the majority of those past sixty." What areas of service would you consider exploring when you retire? What would be the benefits for you? For others?

Looking Good
Blesses
<u>Everybody</u>

[Humanity] looks at the outward appearance,
but the LORD looks at the heart.

1 Samuel 16:7

At the age of sixty, Jane Haas invested seven thousand dollars in plastic surgery to enhance her appearance. Photographs and an explanation appeared in the *Orange County Register.* An inherited collection of skin folds under her chin and on her neck had given her the look of a much older woman. Jane certainly looked older than she acted. A spirited broadcaster and journalist with a pleasant manner, her life is full and challenging. Jane's new look now matches her life as an energetic professional. Her remodeled exterior is congruent with her inner self. I applaud Jane's courage. While not all of us need make such drastic expenditures to improve our appearance, it was right for Jane.

Like it or not, we humans respond to the way people look. That's why looks really do matter. Not to the extent we sometimes think, but significantly. Although God looks at our hearts, people look at our outward appearance. How we look affects the way others think about us. By improving her appearance, Jane gave herself a better chance at being seen for who she really is.

A young man I know is intelligent and highly educated. He dresses in the shabbiest of attire and wears his hair unkempt, complemented by a heavy untrimmed beard. His outward appearance belies his internal qualities. Furthermore, looking at him is not enjoyable. I sometimes wonder if he's ever considered that although he doesn't have to look at himself more than a few seconds a day, others do. Why present unattractiveness to the world when you can offer the opposite?

God loves beauty. Creation sings with glorious colors, incredible sounds, and fantastic shapes. And God created us with spirits that are nourished by the beauty that surrounds us. Being deprived of beauty sickens our soul and erodes our essential humanity. Everyone needs loveliness. So giving this gift to ourselves and others is a noble contribution.

Joyce died after a year-long illness. Exactly one week before her final day she kept an appointment to have her hair washed and styled. Although Joyce knew the end was near, she never wavered from her desire to look her best. This high value for looking good is shared by others—in many senior facilities a weekly appointment for hair care is a highlight in people's schedules. The world is brightened by their care and so are they.

Keeping alive a concern for looking good on into senior years sends a message to the coming generations. It says old is not boring; old is not dead. A neat, stylish, and colorful appearance proclaims, "I am a person. I deserve to be noticed and respected."

Looking good knows no age restrictions. But as the years add up, some of us tighten our purse strings. We may stop buying attractive clothing and eliminate the so-called nonessential expenses. Those who succumb to this inner call for frugality frequently settle into plain, gray practicality. Such an attitude can also signal a giving up on life, a premature dying.

Jane Haas's career as a television personality nudged her into a major expense most of us need not consider. But every one of us can think a little more about looking good for others with only minor embellishments. Paying attention to grooming and a neat appearance is a kind of self-help that causes ripples of benefits to everyone around. God calls us to lifelong thoughtfulness—of ourselves and of others. Presenting a pleasing countenance is an enduring gift—a gift that also affirms our ongoing vitality and value.

Of course, the most important kind of beauty is internal. You can't see it. But God looks at the heart and sees our inner beauty. Coincidentally, a wholesome and integrated soul is usually reflected on the surface.

So cultivate inner beauty, and let your outward appearance reflect what's inside. Experience the joy of blessing those around you.

Questions for Reflection

1. Can you tell what a person is really like by looking at their outward appearance? What message does your own appearance send to others?

2. Inspiring music, creative architecture, a colorful garden, an artistically-presented meal—all are forms of the beauty that surrounds us. What kind of beauty lifts your spirit most? Does a person's physical beauty belong in the same category as these others?

3. "Those who succumb to this inner call for frugality frequently settle into plain, gray practicality." The author states that sometimes this attitude of frugality signals a kind of giving up on life. How can attention to looking good counteract that attitude?

Putting Your
House in Order

"This is what the LORD says:
Put your house in order. . . ."

2 Kings 20:1

My mania for getting rid of things still surprises me. It's a relatively new phenomenon. I wonder if it is age or some unnamed quirk that's just now rising to the surface.

Used books are on the way to the church fund-raiser. Clothing, old suitcases, odd household appliances and fixtures are sorted and ready to be picked up by the Second Time Around store. Stacks of newspaper clippings, notebooks, and Xerox copies of teaching handouts are being whittled to a few essentials. The remainder will go later. Soon. These days, even emptying wastebaskets, straightening the attic, and clearing out decaying boards and stacks of outdoor junk satisfy me.

In many ways, I'm relishing a new sense of mastering my environment. The positive confusion of being a parent to resident youth is long gone; instead the reality of their absence is finally sinking in. The haze of constant financial shortages is clearing; in its place the sun of new affluence shines. I've traded in the feeling of constant busyness for a more manageable schedule. Now I enjoy space, extras, money, time for breathing, looking around, and looking ahead.

Being on top of things is a heady feeling. I change the oil in my car right on time, pay the bills punctually, mow the lawn weekly, go to bed at 9:00 and get up at 5:30 like clockwork. On and on the list stretches, orderly, tidy.

I have to admit, though, I'm also a trifle uneasy about my recent bout of cleaning and straightening. This interlude of relative smooth sailing that's allowed me to regain order in my life worries me. I am able to control my world, or so it seems lately. It makes me nervous. Is this the heart's yearning for a tidy life after decades of relative messiness? Or is it a strong, primeval urge to be in control?

I'm uneasy because of my long-held prejudice against those who tightly and neatly control their world. I'll never forget the childless relatives our family of six occasionally used to visit. Their home was spotless. There was a place for everything, and everything was in its place. Exact routines dictated every activity—how and when to fill the bird feeder, clear and wipe the dinner table, enter and exit the car. Anyone who violated the proper systematic procedures risked incurring verbal scorn or, at the very least, a withering look of disgust.

I also remember my irritation, long ago, with visiting my parents. Each comfortable family time was interrupted, mid-evening, by my father. He'd suddenly get up from his chair and announce he was going to bed. That was it. Non-negotiable. Nothing could sway him from his appointed bedtime. It didn't matter that we were present only on a rare long-distance rendezvous. The clock chimed and the party was over. Dad went to bed.

Being in control is a powerful, intoxicating position we humans don't easily relinquish. So it's probably a good thing that, for many of us, our children steal it from us the moment they make their way into our lives. With the first cry, the first soiled diaper, children drag us, kicking and screaming (we, not they), to our knees. In innocent readiness and oblivious anticipation we tend to their dependency.

This shattering of our sense of control—whether by having children or by some other means—can be spiritually beneficial. It may even be essential for the proper nurture of our souls. Because one of the main dangers in leaving our hunger for control unchecked is that we sacrifice community. We fence people out. We discard important relational responsibilities. As a result, we're left undisturbed and isolated, with the illusion of control.

"Undisturbed" may sometimes sound like a good place to be. But God's people need disturbance. The storms and uncertainties we endure generate a healthy awareness of our vulnerability and dependency on God. We learn compassion, prayer, and reliance on divine assistance best when our lives feel out of control.

It's tempting to organize our lives into cells of isolation and orderliness, eliminating the messiness and feelings of helplessness that disturb us. But those very feelings are essential to developing an empty-handed faith in God.

The notion of control is an illusion anyway. We may order life all we want, dispose of excess, eliminate disruption, cut out clamoring intruders. The thing we cannot master is our own mortality. What we control is minor stuff. Engineering a neat, predictable environment merely distracts us from our ultimate fragility, our inevitable dying, our real vulnerability. Three days ago a special friend of mine suddenly died. A healthy, happy, fifty-three-year-old father, pastor—a great guy. My illusion of control shattered again, this time by an aneurysm.

Jesus told a rich young man to go and sell all his possessions to find eternal life. He saw before him a man whose wealth gave him the illusion of control. Until the rich man willingly reentered the kind of uncertainty his affluence had eliminated, he would not learn to ask the right questions. Only those who are closely in touch with life's chaotic complexity know they need God.

So straightening things up and clearing excess is great— as long as we retain a clear focus on our spiritual neediness. Only God can fix that. Immaculate closets, garages, and attics may provide satisfaction. Diet, exercise, and clean living may stave off physical incapacity. Moving to a gated community may protect us from civic disarray. But human vulnerability and spiritual neediness still wait on God alone.

Questions for Reflection

1. Think of a time when circumstances in your life felt out of control. Did the experience bring you closer to God?

2. Does growing older affect our ability to accept areas of change, disorder, or flexibility in our lives? In your experience has such acceptance become easier? More difficult?

3. To what extent is the notion of control an illusion? Are there some areas of life you are able to control? Is this positive or negative for your spiritual well-being?

Greener Pastures
<u>Look Inviting</u>

*"Go, walk through the length and breadth
of the land, for I am giving it to you."*

Genesis 13:17

When retired friends announced that they were moving on to greener pastures, I did my best to generate appropriate excitement on their behalf. Really I was worried. Sad too. Because watching friends leave is hard. The main source of my worry, though, comes from what I've observed over the years. I've seen too many lives broken by canny moves to warmer climates or great real estate opportunities in distant places.

Don't get me wrong. Zillions of people migrate success-fully. They may congratulate themselves daily on their decision to leave home for a new place. But a half-zillion never regain the zest and satisfactions they left behind. They suffer. And half of both groups deny their losses, never admitting, even to themselves, their regrets and grief. Denial is easier.

Sometimes evidence of the downside to pulling up stakes and starting over sneaks in in the form of illness. That happened to Rose. A lifelong resident of California, Rose and her husband couldn't resist the temptation of wonderful housing deals in Nevada. The idea of lush, inexpensive golf courses at their back door beckoned. So they moved to a house twice the size of the one they sold and pocketed the change.

It took a year and a half to get the house furnished the way they wanted it and the yard groomed to their satisfaction. Then they prepared to settle into serious retirement leisure. But right around the time the challenges of putting together their new residence tapered down, Rose fell ill. Two years later, her bereft husband called about funeral arrangements.

It's true that illness can strike us anytime, whether we've lived in one home all our lives or just made a major move. But notice what happens to those who pack up and leave the comfort zone they've built up over a lifetime—a network of resources and suppliers, a nest of caring and concerned loved ones. In some cases, at least, the body registers such disruption as a serious loss. And serious loss of any kind can lower immunity and undermine health. Some people never recover from the effects of a radical departure from familiar places and people. The body keeps score.

Most people know there's far more to life than sunny weather or a spacious home. But those aren't the only attractions that lure seniors away from established homes. It's easy succumb to the lure of another, related enticement that's often fraught with pitfalls: leaving home to reside in a distant place where sons and daughters live.

Helen and Ben did that. In frequent phone conversations, week after week, their daughter pleaded with them to move closer to her. After they retired, finally free from the confinement of full-time employment, Helen and Ben said yes. Dearly loved grandchildren added to the attraction. They could see no solid reason standing in the way. So off they went.

It took them a year to realize their mistake. They quickly discovered that their adult children had "a life" in that place that did not, and could not, conveniently include them very much. Their expectation of weekly activities and full fellowship with their children was soon trimmed down to little more than occasional holiday get-togethers. At the same time, caring for their grandchildren became a chore instead of a joy as Helen and Ben began to feel taken for granted. Finding compatible friends proved easier said than done. They ached over the loss of the comfortable relationships they'd left behind.

As Helen and Ben began to admit their dilemma, their frustration oozed to the surface. Now they felt trapped: returning to their former hometown was not a realistic option; staying looked too difficult. Fortunately, Ben and Helen eventually carved out a satisfying life in their new place. In the end, proximity to their grandchildren and children made it worthwhile. But their story raises a beacon of caution to those who entertain fantasies of greener pastures in far-off places.

On the positive side, major life changes can also be invigorating. Meeting new people and experiencing new places stimulate fresh thinking. The stretching, accommodating, and expanding they require of us evoke excitement and satisfaction. Many people have discovered that change can be deeply rejuvenating. Those who accept no challenges, create no fresh tests of their capacities, and move only in old routines may be the stalest of souls. That's not to say there is something wrong with folks who change rarely, slowly, or even not at all. Like those who thrive on variety, these folks own a legitimate style.

However, trouble may arise when one of each kind of person needs to reach a mutual decision that affects both. It is no surprise that it's easy for two like-spirited people to make major decisions about change together. More often, though, opposites attract, which escalates the complexity of their decision-making. When one partner pushes for change while the other digs in, frustration is sure to follow.

I counseled a couple who were debating a radical move to a Hawaiian island. Sally found it a wildly exciting prospect. Don approached it with apprehension. After much debate, Don finally conceded, "OK. I'll go for your sake, but I still feel shaky about leaving the mainland." I didn't feel comfortable with this conclusion. "You need to reach a point," I suggested, "where you both recognize the negatives and together embrace the positives. Otherwise you're setting yourselves up for a lot of 'I told you so' arguments. When you face the difficulties and the benefits hand-in-hand, you'll be ready to decide." Recognizing and acknowledging the positives as well as the negatives of every situation lays a firm foundation for good decision-making.

Unlike our parents, we live in a time of mobility and opportunity. Choices abound. Experiences once available only to the very rich—travel, a major move to another part of the country—are accessible to many people. More than ever, the choices we face require prayer, thoughtfulness, and a careful weighing of gains and losses. Heading for greener pastures without recognizing the mountains we first have to cross promises unexpected setbacks. But with God's help, we can climb every mountain—whether it be on our way to a distant place or in our own backyard.

Questions for Reflection

1. For what reasons would you consider packing up and leaving your home territory, friends, and even family? List the positives and negatives of such a move.

2. How can "facing the difficulties and the benefits hand-in-hand" help couples make a decision about a major life change?

3. Many adult children live far away from their parents. Think of ways for parents and their children and grandchildren to maintain a meaningful relationship (short of moving to the same town).

How a Garage Sale Wrecked Christmas

There is a time for everything,
and a season for every activity under heaven: . . .
a time to keep and a time to throw away . . .

Ecclesiastes 3:1, 6

After the dust settled in our new home in Southern California fifteen years ago, we discovered that we had no place for a lot of the odds and ends we'd accumulated over the years. We decided to solve the problem by organizing our first and only garage sale. By Saturday noon we were assured of success. We had consolidated our spread of disposable items onto two medium-size tables, compared to six when we started. The remainder could go to the thrift shop.

A couple of years later I felt some regret over one item we sold for a pittance that day—my large, upright Underwood typewriter, vintage 1930. I had hammered out about three hundred sermons and scores of articles on the heavy black machine, now rendered obsolete by my personal computer and printer. No longer of any use to me, it had nevertheless evolved in my mind into an object of affection, an artifact with nostalgic significance.

I wished I still had it to remind me of times past—intense times, draining times, and the powerful, exhilarating times when ideas flew onto the paper.

Something else got sold that Saturday morning, but I never missed it—until the following Christmas. When our adult daughter arrived from Michigan, she noticed right away. "Where is our old manger scene?" she wanted to know. My wife and I had not expected this reaction. A year earlier, we'd purchased a beautiful new, yes elegant, crèche to replace the dingy K-mart set we'd lived with for the previous twenty years. The new manger scene looked handsome and expensive—in our minds, a giant step up from the old one.

Alas, Julie paid scant notice to this wonderful acquisition and offered no praise. She wanted the crèche she'd grown up with. When one of us told her about the garage-sale fate of her beloved manger scene, the harsh news registered as totally unacceptable. To this day, a decade and a half later, an occasional needle darts our way for the thoughtless, unfeeling disposal of a precious icon.

Sooner or later, everybody does it. My dad, for instance, has given away dozens of things I'd like to have. Such unthinking actions are caused by empathy deficit. One generation fails to realize the attachments felt by the younger generation to certain household items. What's "old stuff" to parents can be objects of sentimental value to their children. One generation's throwaways are "keepers" for the kids who grew up handling them, playing with them, or even just looking at them.

I remember well three or four hundred Indian Head pennies my dad had collected and kept in the back of one of his desk drawers. As a little kid, I loved rummaging through Dad's keepsakes and playing with them. He probably didn't know I liked them because I never told him. Years passed, and suddenly I was an adult savoring nostalgic times and objects. "What ever happened to your Indian Head pennies?" I asked one visit. "I gave them to somebody who collects coins," Dad calmly reported. "He asked if he could have them." "Oh," I said, somewhat bewildered. Of course they belonged to Dad, I thought. He had the right to do with them as he pleased. I had never asked for them or even let him know I was fond of them. Still, it felt like I had unfairly lost something dear.

Managing the inevitable losses of such family memorabilia without bitterness and resentment requires some kind of resolution. I resolved not to let the loss of objects undermine family love. Relationships are too precious to let material things, no matter how valuable, undermine them. Allowing family harmony to erode because our nostalgia is violated is foolish and wrong. At the same time, it's worth resolving to avoid thoughtless housecleaning. Sweeping with too broad a broom can be unnecessarily hurtful.

For Julie the cheap little manger scene was a reservoir of childhood daydreams about the original Christmas. Time spent moving and carefully placing the shepherds, Joseph, the cow, and the sheep made real and vivid for her that first holy night. We didn't notice the depth of the relationship. To us it was a Christmas decoration, plain and simple, finally discarded as our affluence allowed a step up.

"There is a time for everything," said the preacher, "and a season for every activity under heaven: . . . a time to keep and a time to throw away . . ." Sometimes it's difficult to discern which time is which. But it's always worth remembering, as God's children, that a little extra caution may prevent more than a few tears.

Questions for Reflection

1. What object(s) from your past do you wish you still had? What happened to it? What made it valuable to you?

2. The author claims that "an empathy deficit" accounts for the casting off of objects our loved ones value. What are some ways to avoid such thoughtless actions?

3. "Relationships are too precious to let material things, no matter what they are, undermine them." How will you avoid allowing objects (or their loss) stand between you and the people you love?

I Don't Get Around Much Anymore

A cheerful heart is good medicine. . . .

Proverbs 17:22

A cheerful heart is good medicine," Proverbs teaches us. But even the most lighthearted older folks get let down by bodily weakness. Eventually we all must cope with physical limitations.

Shortly after my fiftieth birthday, I gave up serious competitive tennis. My aggressive nature spurred me into playing so intensely that I barely recovered in time for the next week's match. My spirit was willing, but my flesh was too weak. At that point, good sense called for age-appropriate behavior modification. Now I play golf.

The truth is, the physical changes of aging involve some grief. A sudden loss of physical well-being will be accompanied by intense grief. On the other hand, when our limitations ease in gradually, our grief is likely to be mild. I lament the slow erosion of my physical stamina and resilience, but only a little. New challenges have captured my attention. For the present, at least, I'm satisfied with manageable alternatives. Walking is as good as jogging.

Gardening satisfies my soul more than racquetball ever did.

When my father reached eighty his driver's license was renewed. He just barely passed the vision test. Dad knew this would be his final driving stint. "I have four more years to live," he prophesied. Clearly he was apprehensive about what would happen to him when he could no longer drive. Anticipating the shrinkage of his world four years down the road was painful for him. Today Dad is ninety-six, in his twelfth non-driving year. He's discovered that there is life even after driving days are done.

Mother's physical letdown involves her hearing. At ninety-one, she hears little that is not spoken right in her face at peak volume. This shortcoming has eliminated the possibility of relaxed conversation. It leaves her on the perimeter of lively fellowship. For Mother, attending church no longer holds joy, only frustration. She seldom goes. Her failing ability to hear has radically downsized her world. Most of the time she feels left out and alone. Her spirit is waning. Experiencing what it's like for my mother to be deaf has made me revise my thinking about comparing this loss with blindness. I used to think that, given a choice, I would give up hearing before seeing. Blindness seemed a greater loss by far than deafness. I've since changed my mind. As I see it, blindness cuts people off from the delights of objects. Deafness hedges out relationships. That is, the loss of vision eliminates things; the loss of hearing takes away people. Which is more necessary to maintaining a healthy spirit? It seems to me that fellowship with others is far more vital to our souls than enjoying the delights of objects.

In our culture, postponing physical loss is a major preoccupation. It always has been. The search for a fountain of youth is deeply embedded in human history. Today much of the search takes place in the laboratories of major universities and pharmaceutical industries. Right now we know a number of factors in that elusive fountain. The most obvious discoveries involve eating a healthy diet and getting enough exercise. Other lifestyle choices or behaviors—such as abstaining from smoking and using automobile seatbelts—can make a major difference too. Conscientious attention to these known lifesavers can add years to our lives.

Nevertheless, "postponing" is the operative word here. Physical weakening is an inevitable part of growing old. The writer of Ecclesiastes paints a picture of what happens when we are old:

> Remember your Creator
> in the days of your youth,
> before the days of trouble come
> and the years approach when you will say,
> "I find no pleasure in them"—
> before the sun and the light
> and the moon and the stars grow dark,
> and the clouds return after the rain;
> when the keepers of the house tremble,
> and the strong men stoop,
> when the grinders cease because they are few,
> and those looking through the windows grow dim . . .
> and desire no longer is stirred.
> —Ecclesiastes 12:1-3, 5

I once irritated a small group of seminary students by proclaiming that they would never find me in a nursing home. They thought my statement was preposterous. "That's what happens to old people," they cried. "You can't decide about it. It happens!" Actually, only about 5 percent of the aged need such care. Statistical probability favors no such destiny. For myself, I pledge to drink of the fountain of youth to enhance my odds for a long and active life.

Today God blesses us daily with health-enhancing discoveries. We can choose to participate in them—by getting flu shots, by getting enough rest and exercise, by conscientiously nurturing our souls—or we can pass them by. Taking good care of ourselves offers more than postponing the inevitable funeral. By staying healthy and active long into our senior years, we multiply our opportunities to serve and support others. We have the opportunity to participate fully in God's mandate for a longer span of time.

"A cheerful heart is good medicine. . . ." And a happy and healthy octogenarian sets a positive standard, encouraging all of us to lift the bar higher. That senior citizen represents the kingdom of God growing and blessing our world.

Questions for Reflection

1. Do you agree that the losses of deafness may be more painful than the losses of blindness? How do these and other physical losses affect our spiritual life?

2. The author says, "I pledge to drink of the fountain of youth." To what extent can we control our physical well-being as we grow older? Think of some positive steps you can take to stay as healthy as possible.

3. How do you feel about people who seem to ignore life-enhancing practices? How do you think God feels about them?

Let Heaven Wait

For to me, to live is Christ and to die is gain.

Philippians 1:21

I n one of my early memories, my father is preaching, fervently paraphrasing words from Revelation 22, "Come, Lord Jesus. Come quickly." Even as a youngster, this urgent plea always bothered me. There was so much fun to be enjoyed, so much life to be lived. I had no interest in a dramatic life change—even of the most glorious kind.

Dad's fervent use of those biblical words in his preaching convinced me that for him, the reality of facing the end of life on earth would come easily. His eagerness about the prospect of meeting the Lord, either through a second coming or physical death, never did sit well with me, however. To this day, life as I know it is the highest priority. Life with Christ, later, is a consolation. It removes the sharpest sting from death, but it's not something I long for with my Dad's fervor.

Recently Father flirted with death. Not for the first time—but this time, maybe because of his advanced age, he felt like this certainly was the end. His reluctance about meeting the Lord surprised me. So I asked him directly: "Is it alright with you to move on to the next life?" I fully anticipated an affirmative reply. "Come, Lord Jesus . . ." echoed in my memory. "No," he answered, "I'd rather stay here a little longer."

Dad did recover and soon resumed his daily walks. To my mind, he'd revealed his true colors. My early memories conflicted sharply with the present reality of Dad fighting for life and enjoying each new day.

Gladys was diagnosed with leukemia only six months after her husband's sudden death. Doctors recommended drastic treatments; they told her that her life was in great jeopardy. But Gladys declined the medical efforts proposed. For one thing, she knew the treatments were not a sure thing. But the real reason for her decision, she said, was the prospect of rejoining her husband, with the Lord. She allowed the illness to run its course and died peacefully about the time the doctors had predicted.

Part of me admires Gladys's courage. On the other hand, I am uncomfortable that an idea like meeting her husband again would hold such convincing power. Gladys's hope—filled guess was based on biblical hints, but the exact substance of what is to come after our physical death is very cloudy.

Facing certain death serenely is admirable. Even the courage to choose quality of life over the ravages of life-lengthening treatments is impressive. But when religion deals with the profound mystery of life after death by painting such a clear picture of a heavenly family reunion that people give up on their life here on earth, something is wrong.

You've probably heard the expression "The mind focuses well when facing a firing squad." My father found out what he really believed when he was under the gun. Gladys did too. But Gladys's outlook was too much colored, I think, by the way we Christians talk these days about seeing loved ones in heaven.

The apostle Paul said, "For to me, to live is Christ and to die is gain." This sounds like "Six of one, a half dozen of the other." In other words, Paul pictures both as being positive. He desires neither more strongly than the other. Life as we know it, in the body, is God's first plan for us. Life here is not an inferior existence. It is not merely to be tolerated or endured like some temporary hard labor sentence. "Cherished," "spent," "appreciated," "invested in," "enjoyed," are more appropriate words than "endured." We should not tolerate eagerness to leave this life without overwhelmingly good arguments.

No one should be embarrassed about wanting to live long. A longing to depart this life is not spiritually superior to reluctance. Life is a gift to be used and embraced until the body breaks down irreparably. Then letting go finally fits.

On the other hand, now and then Christians hang on to this life longer than they should. Hazel's husband, Herb, went down with a massive stroke. Medical assessments of his prognosis were gloomy to hopeless. If he recovered at all, the doctors said, at best he'd be left with little awareness of his surroundings and no ability to communicate. But Hazel was a woman of strong faith. She was unwavering in her confidence that a miracle would prove all medical predictions incorrect. She rallied prayer groups. Still Herb's condition showed no gains. The family was advised to discontinue artificial support as Herb's body bloated with retained fluids. But Hazel would not give in. Finally Herb's body was awfully distorted. After many days of waiting, no encouraging signs of consciousness appeared. At last, reluctantly, Hazel conceded.

When to say "enough" will always be a judgment call. But I think Hazel hung on too long. There is more to life than our physical bodies. Our belief that a wondrous, albeit mysterious, transition awaits us ought to make it a little bit easier—though never easy—to let go when life comes to an end. This hope can rightly help us to loosen our grip when the body fails. Coming to the end of our lives or the lives of the ones we love is a serious loss. But as the apostle Paul says, we grieve "not like those who have no hope."

As for me, when my journey comes to an end, I hope my loving family members struggle hard with letting me go. However, I am troubled by the thought of them acting like shrieking pagans for whom life is a one-way, dead-end road. Rather, I hope their gracious love tearfully begrudges my departure, while the living Christ enables them to relax their firm grip and let go. And when I'm gone, I hope they'll grieve, but not like those who have no hope.

Questions for Reflection

1. Do you think it's appropriate for Christians to eagerly anticipate heaven? Why or why not?

2. Can strong confidence in a life-saving miracle ever be misguided? How can we tell when it's time to "let go"?

3. According to the author, Paul's saying "To live is Christ and to die is gain" means that both are equally positive. What implications does this have for how we live? How we die?

4. Some people insist that there be no crying at their funeral, only celebration. Is that a realistic option?